"Be responsible for the fish in the sea,

the birds in the air, the cattle, and,

yes, Earth itself, and every animal that

moves on the face of Earth."

Genesis 1:26, MESSAGE

"What a wildly wonderful world, God! You made it all,

with Wisdom at your side, made earth overflow with

your wonderful creations. . . ."

Psalm 104:24, MESSAGE

Let's Explore God's World

"G'day, mate!"

Written & Illustrated by

Debby Anderson

CROSSWAY BOOKS • WHEATON, IL

Dear Grown-up Readers,

In the beginning, God gave us the responsibility
of caring for His brand-new world. As our generation
passes on this responsibility to the next, there is a sense
of urgency. We hope this little book will help to develop
a sense of joyful hope in all of us. Let's get outside!

Isaiah 11:6–9; Hosea 4:1–3; 6:3; 14:4–9

Prayerfully,
Debby Anderson

A special thanks to HUNG, Mai, owner of the Pho Saigon Restaurant and to my
young artists: Luke Lund, Shawntell Smith, Chloe Snyder, Vitaliy Stefanyuk.

Let's Explore God's World
Copyright © 2009 by Debby Anderson
Published by Crossway Books
        a publishing ministry of Good News Publishers
        1300 Crescent Street
        Wheaton, Illinois 60187

Editor: LB Norton. Designer: Keane Fine
First printing 2009
Printed in the United States of America
Scripture references marked MESSAGE are from The Message. Copyright © by Eugene H. Peterson 1993, 1994, 1995, 1996, 2000, 2001, 2002. Used by permission of NavPress Publishing Group.

Scripture references marked NLT are from The Holy Bible, New Living Translation, copyright © 1996. Used by permission of Tyndale House Publishers, Inc., Wheaton, IL, 60189. All rights reserved.

Hardback ISBN: 978-1-4335-0708-3
PDF ISBN: 978-1-4335-0709-0
Mobipocket ISBN: 978-1-4335-0710-6

Library of Congress Cataloging-in-Publication Data
Anderson, Debby.
  Let's explore God's world / written and Illustrated by Debby Anderson.
    p. cm.
  ISBN 978-1-4335-0708-3 (hc)
  1. Nature—Religious aspects—Christianity—Juvenile literature. 2. Creation—Juvenile literature. I. Title.

BT695.5.A53 2009
231.7'65—dc22   2008044113

L B   18   17   16   15   14   13   12   11   10   09
14   13   12   11   10   9   8   7   6   5   4   3   2   1

For Dad and Mom Dryden
and Dad and Mom Anderson.
You were the first ones to help us
explore God's world!
Love, Debby and Family

God made our wide wonderful world. He filled it with bird eggs and bug legs . . .

leaves and laughter . . .

. . . rainbows and rhinos!

Psalm 89:11; Genesis 9:13

God also made our senses so we can explore His world!

He made our ears
for hearing . . .

eyes for seeing . . .

fingers for
feeling . . .

tongues for tasting . . .

Psalm 34:8; 139:13; Matthew 13:16

. . . and noses for smelling!
With our senses, we can learn all
about God's world. Let's go exploring!

Genesis 1:26–31; 2:15; Job 12:7–13; Psalm 8:6–8

The more we learn about God's world, the more we want to take care of it! Look for the butterfly and the **R** words that help us to be **responsible!**

Along the beach . . .
We see God's wisdom in the shapes of shells and wiggly-jiggly jellyfish.
We feel warm sand beneath our bare feet and sunshine all around.
We taste the sea's salty spray and smell the slippery seaweed.
In the roar and rush of the waves, we hear God's power
. . . and God hears us!

Psalm 116:1–2; 148:7

Reduce! Turn off the water! The less water we use, the less water comes out of the oceans, rivers, and lakes!

In the woods . . .
God is with us as we walk along. We feel His
peace in the calm coolness of the shade.
We smell fallen leaves and see scampering
squirrels and roly-poly raccoons.
We hear the chatter of chipmunks and chickadees.
We taste blackberries, blueberries, raspberries,
and huckleberries.

Proverbs 3:6; Psalm 121:5–8

Reduce! Because paper comes from trees, the less paper we throw away, the fewer trees are cut down. Fill your paper with writing and drawing. **Reuse** the scraps for another project! **Reuse** tubes and boxes!

Ephesians 2:10

In the city . . .
We see sunrises and sunsets.
We hear talking and traffic, beeping and buses.
We smell and taste tamales and tacos and oodles of noodles!

Job 38:12; Psalm 104:19

COMMUNITY
MARKET

We feel God's love in the hugs and
homes of our families and friends!

1 John 3:1; 4:19

In the rain forest . . .
We feel bushy vines and mushy moss.
We see God's creativity in bugs and beetles, frogs and polliwogs.
We hear macaws and monkeys, toucans and toads!
We smell and taste papaya and pineapple!
We wonder how a creepy-crawly caterpillar changes
into a beautiful butterfly.

Genesis 1; Proverbs 6:6

Respect the animals and
be gentle with them.

In the desert . . .
We feel prickly cactus and windblown sand.
We see the colors of the rocks and desert fox.
We hear coyotes howl and owls hoot.
We smell and taste peppery pots of spicy rice!
We thank God for food!

Job 39:19; Isaiah 35:1–2

In the garden . . .
We see God's gift of life growing all around us.
We feel soft squishy soil and sparkly sunshine.
We taste tiny tangy tomatoes.
We hear buzzing bees and smell big bright beautiful blossoms.
We wonder how a tiny seed grows into a giant sunflower.

Psalm 104:14, 30

Renew! Plant seeds for new plants!

On the mountain . . .
We feel cold sparkly snow and smell evergreen trees.
We taste the snacks from our backpacks.
We see God's might in the height of the cliffs.
We hear the cry of the eagle as it soars in the sky.

Job 39:27; Psalm 95:4; Philippians 4:4

Rejoice! Enjoy a hike!
Collect rocks!
Take a picture!

At the park . . .
We feel the whoosh of the wind as we run and ride.
We smell the green grass below and hear the birds above.
We munch our lunch!
We see our friends . . . and God sees us!

Psalm 33:13; 147:8

Recycle! Help make old things into new things! Be responsible!

Everywhere we go, we can use our
senses to explore God's world!
What can we see? Smell? Taste? Touch? Hear?

Job 12:7–10; Psalm 50:10